Smiling Sushi Roll

スマイリング
スシ
ロール

Tama-chan

たまちゃんのにっこり寿司

 ## はじめに

日々親しんでいるモノのなかに、「おもしろい」ことはまだまだたくさんあるはず。
誰でも知っているけど、誰もが出来ない表現ってなんだろうと、ボンヤリ考えていました。

便利になった現代の日本では、「巻き寿司」は食べたことはあっても
作ったことはない人が多く、私もその一人でした。
ある時、断面に絵柄が現れる巻き寿司を見て、
「巻き寿司で自由に絵が描けたらおもしろいのでは？」と思い、作ってみました。

しかしいざやってみると、酢飯の量や具材の切り方、パーツの配置、巻き上げるときの力の入れ方で、
イメージしていた絵柄から、どんどん離れていってしまう。
でもそのうち、「コントロールし難い」ことで、かえって対象に近づけるような気がしてきたのです。

いまでも、思ってもみなかった線や形が切り口に現れるのを見るたびに、みなさんと一緒に驚き、楽しんでいます。
そして「食べる」。

そんな巻き寿司作品を、「作ってにっこり、見てにっこり、食べてにっこり」の「にっこり寿司」と命名しました。

これからも「食べられるアート」としてメッセージを込め、
ごはんとのりで、常識や思い込みに一石を投じられたらと思っています。

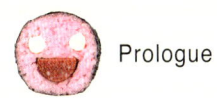 Prologue

There must still be a lot of "hidden interesting things" in what we experience in everyday life.
I was wondering about my own original style through using familiar images which everyone knows.

In a convenient modern country like Japan where you can buy anything in a shop, and even though people have eaten a Sushi Roll, few people including me have made it themselves. One day, I saw a Sushi Roll with a pattern on the surface and thought it would be very interesting if I could draw freely on that surface. So, I tried.

But when I actually started to make the Sushi Roll, I found that the pattern on the surface stepped away from my expectation. This was because its construction depends on the volume of vinegared rice, the way of cutting the ingredients, the layout of the ingredients, the pressure applied when rolling and so on. Meanwhile, I began to think that overcoming the very "uncontrollability" in drawing patterns actually leads to coming close to meeting my goals.

Even now, we are enjoying being surprised by unexpected lines and shapes emerging on the cut surface.
Then we "eat it."

As a result of this process I named these entertaining Sushi Rolls as the "Smiling Sushi Roll" which has the message of "making it with a smile, viewing it with a smile, and eating it with a smile."

While I will promote an "edible art" made of rice and seaweed,
I will continue challenging common knowledge and conventional ideas.

Tama-chan

"神に見放された者は自らの手で運をつかめ"

"God helps those who help themselves"

オーギュスト・ロダン「考える人」より
"The Thinker" by Auguste Rodin

グスタフ・クリムト「接吻」より
"The Kiss" by Gustav Klimt

『にっこり寿司』は、一本ののり巻きの中で色が変わったり、動きが加わったりしてストーリーが生まれることも。だから切るたびに驚きは増し、見ている人の歓声は大きくなってゆくのです。

The uniqueness of the "Smiling Sushi Roll" is that a sushi surface emerges with a different pattern each time you cut unlike a normal Sushi Roll. The Sushi Roll sometimes spins a story by changing color and pattern.

エドヴァルド・ムンク「叫び」より
"The Scream" by Edvard Munch

スペイン旅行の思い出

地面からニョキニョキ生えて来たようなデザインは
人工物であることを忘れてしまいそう。
私の巻き寿司もグニャグニャ、ニョキニョキしているけど
「まっすぐ、キッチリしてないからいい」と言われる。
みんな、心が広いな〜。

Memory of my travel in Spain

The building whose design emerges from the ground and almost makes me forget that it's a man-made object. My Sushi Roll shapes are sometimes imperfect. But they get praise because "they are not too exact." Everyone has such a big heart.

アントニ・ガウディ「サグラダ・ファミリア」より
"Sagrada Família" by Antoni Gaudí

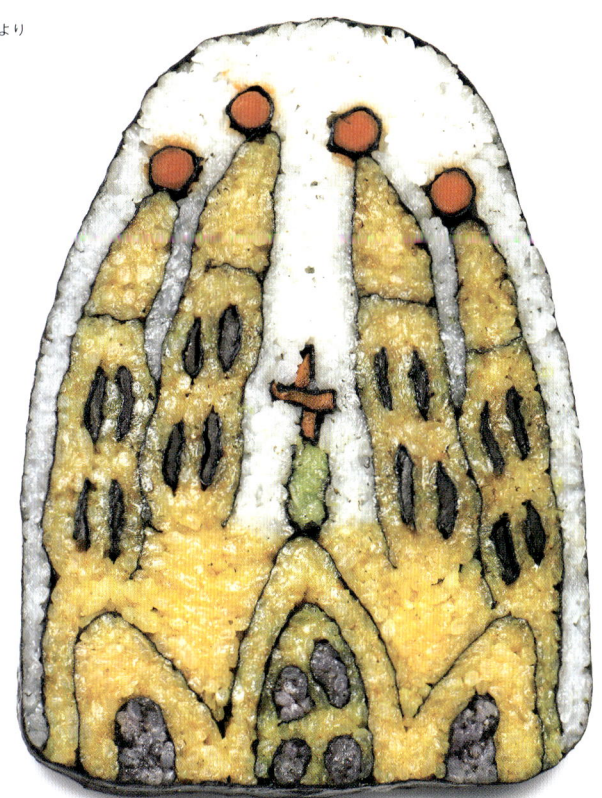

イタリア旅行の思い出

ピサの斜塔って傾いたから観光名所になったよね。
人だって何でも出来て完璧な人より、
ちょっとクセがある人に魅力を感じることの方が多い。
この塔だって、みんな思わず支えたくなっちゃうし。
私はナースで支えてみました。
あ、ピサには行ったことないけどね。

Memory of my journey in Italy
The Leaning Tower of Pisa became a popular tourist destination because of its slant. A person is also the same. A striking person is more attractive than the perfect person who can manage everything well. You might feel like supporting this unique leaning tower. But, I have never been there yet.

It is not only a man who disguises himself.

変装するのは男だけじゃない。

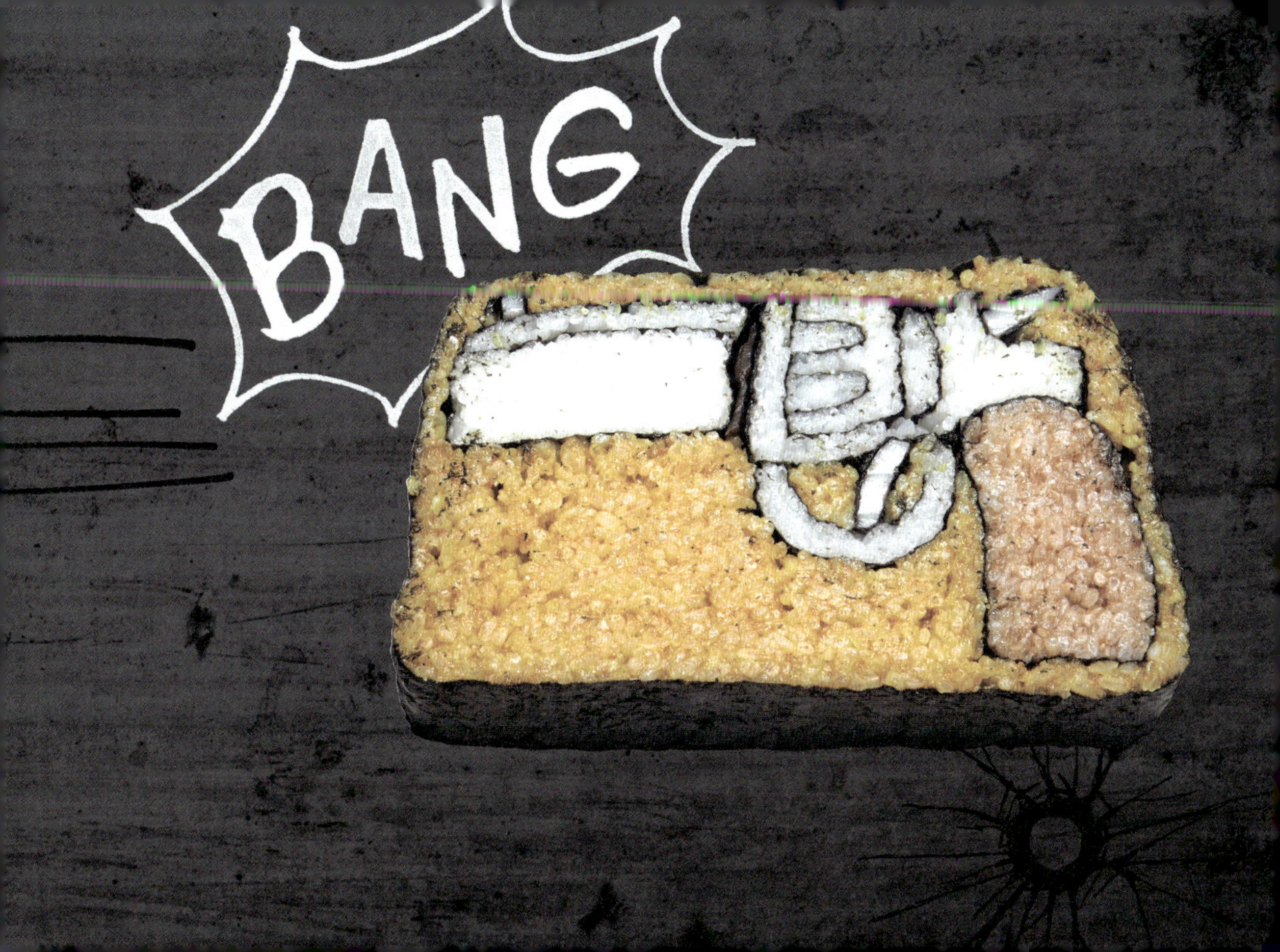
BANG

My Japan
私の好きなニッポン

「宝誌和尚立像」より
The *Houshiwajo* standing figure

顔が割れて中から…

From inside of its face...

宝誌和尚立像を京都の博物館で初めて見た時、ビックリした。ふざけている！
いえ、ふざけているわけではなく「人は内面に神仏が宿る」という意味が込められて中から阿弥陀如来が現れているところらしい。

宝誌和尚は風狂の僧で、一休さんのように常人の域を超えた中国の和尚さん。こんなふうに後世に伝えられるなんて、宝誌和尚っておちゃめな人だったみたい。ステキだね！

I was surprised when I saw the *Houshiwajo* standing figure. Maybe you can't believe it, but the figure's meaning is that "the gods inhabit humans." So, the face of the figure has a crack, and the *Amida* Buddha is coming out.

Houshiwajo was a maverick Chinese monk like Monk *Ikkyu* who had special ideas beyond an ordinary person. Maybe *Houshiwajo* was a unique person as his stories have been passed on from generation to generation. Fantastic!

お米をお米で巻いてみた。

Roll "rice" with rice.

あこがれの江戸時代

浮世絵の中の花魁も映画やドラマに出て来る侍や忍者も今はいない。
でも海外では今でもいると思われていたり。
私達は本物の侍も忍者も花魁も見たことってないけど、
江戸時代には確かに存在した。
アイドルもセレブもスターもいた江戸時代って、
とんでもなく楽しそうだな〜と思う。

A longing for the Edo Period

Neither the *Oirans* in *Ukiyoe* paintings, nor the *Ninjas* you see in a movie or soap opera exist nowadays.
But, some people in other countries believe they still exist.
Although we haven't seen real *Samurais*, *Ninjas*, or *Oirans*, they did indeed exist in the Edo Period.
I imagine the Edo Period where idols, celebrities, and stars lived was unbelievably amusing.

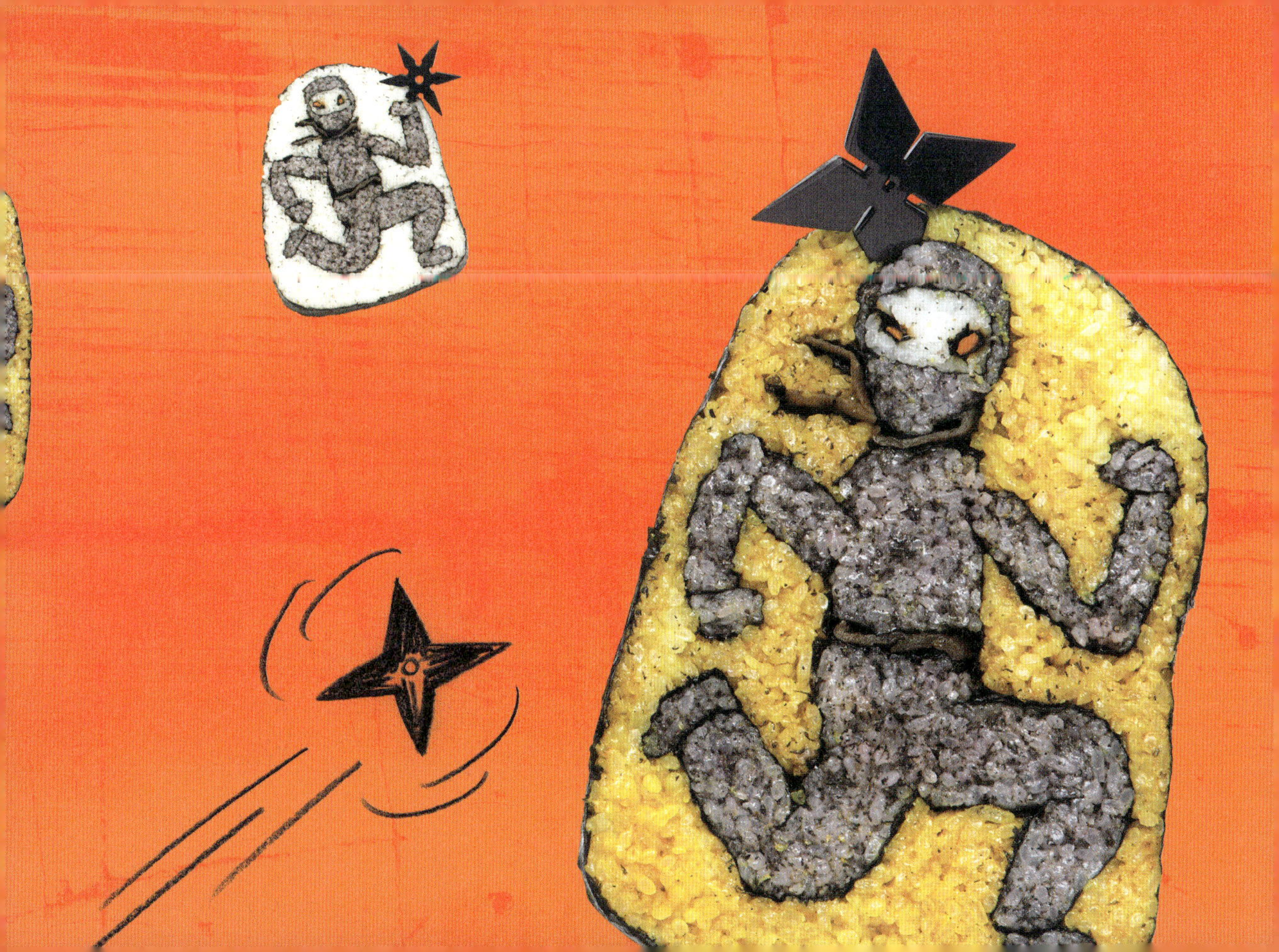

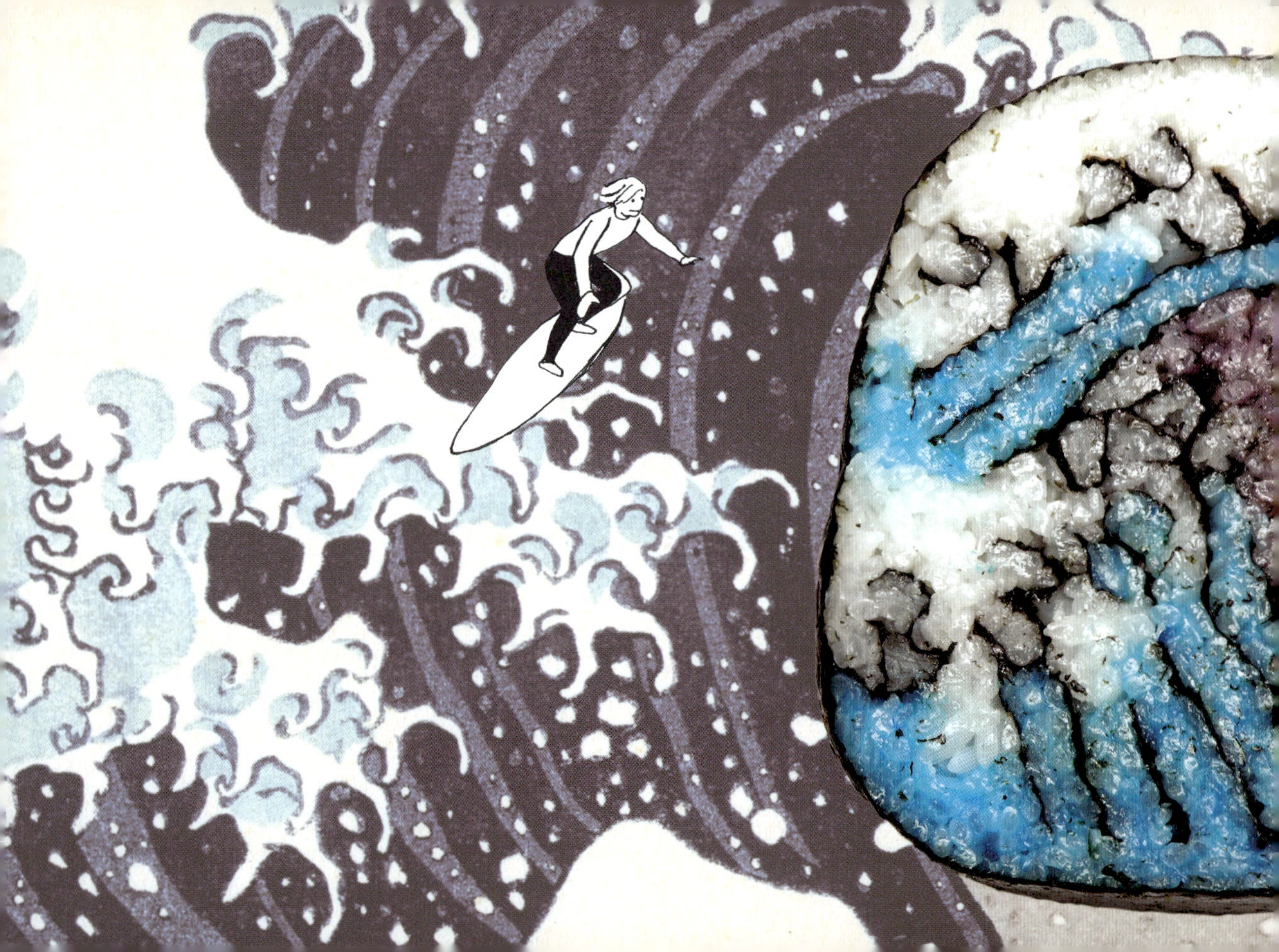

読者ハガキ

151-0051
東京都渋谷区千駄ヶ谷3-56-6

(株)リトルモア 行

Little More

ご住所 〒

お名前(フリガナ)

ご職業　□男　□女

メールアドレス　　　　　　　　　　　才

リトルモアからの新刊・イベント情報を希望　□する　□しない

※ご記入いただきました個人情報は、所定の目的以外には使用しません。

小土の本は全国どこの書店からもお取り寄せが可能です。

http://www.littlemore.co.jp/

[Little More WEBオンラインストア]ですべての書籍がご購入頂けます。
クレジットカード、代金引換がご利用になれます。
税込1,500円以上のお買い上げで送料(300円)が無料になります。
但し、代金引換をご利用の場合、別途、代引手数料がかかります。

ご購読ありがとうございました。
今後の資料とさせていただきますので
アンケートにご協力をお願いいたします。

voice

お買い上げの書名

ご購入書店

　　　　　　　　　市・区・町・村　　　　　　　書店

本書をお求めになった動機は何ですか。
- [ ] 新聞・雑誌などの書評記事を見て（媒体名　　　　）
- [ ] 新聞・雑誌などの広告を見て
- [ ] 友人からすすめられて
- [ ] 店頭で見て
- [ ] ホームページを見て
- [ ] 著者のファンだから
- [ ] その他（　　　　　　　　　　　　　　　　）

最近購入された本は何ですか。（書名　　　　　　　）

本書についてのご感想をお聞かせ下されば、うれしく思います。
小社へのご意見・ご要望などもお書き下さい。

ご協力ありがとうございました。

伝説の
BIG WAVE

葛飾北斎「神奈川沖浪裏」より
"The Great Wave off Kanagawa" by Hokusai

「はじめまして」
"Nice to meet you."

「お世話になります」
"Nice to meet you too."

Japanese salaryman

サラリーマン ジャパニーズ

「●×商事の山田です」
"I'm Yamada working for the ●× trading company."

「▲■物産の田中です」
"I'm Tanaka working for the ▲■ corporation."

EROS
エロス

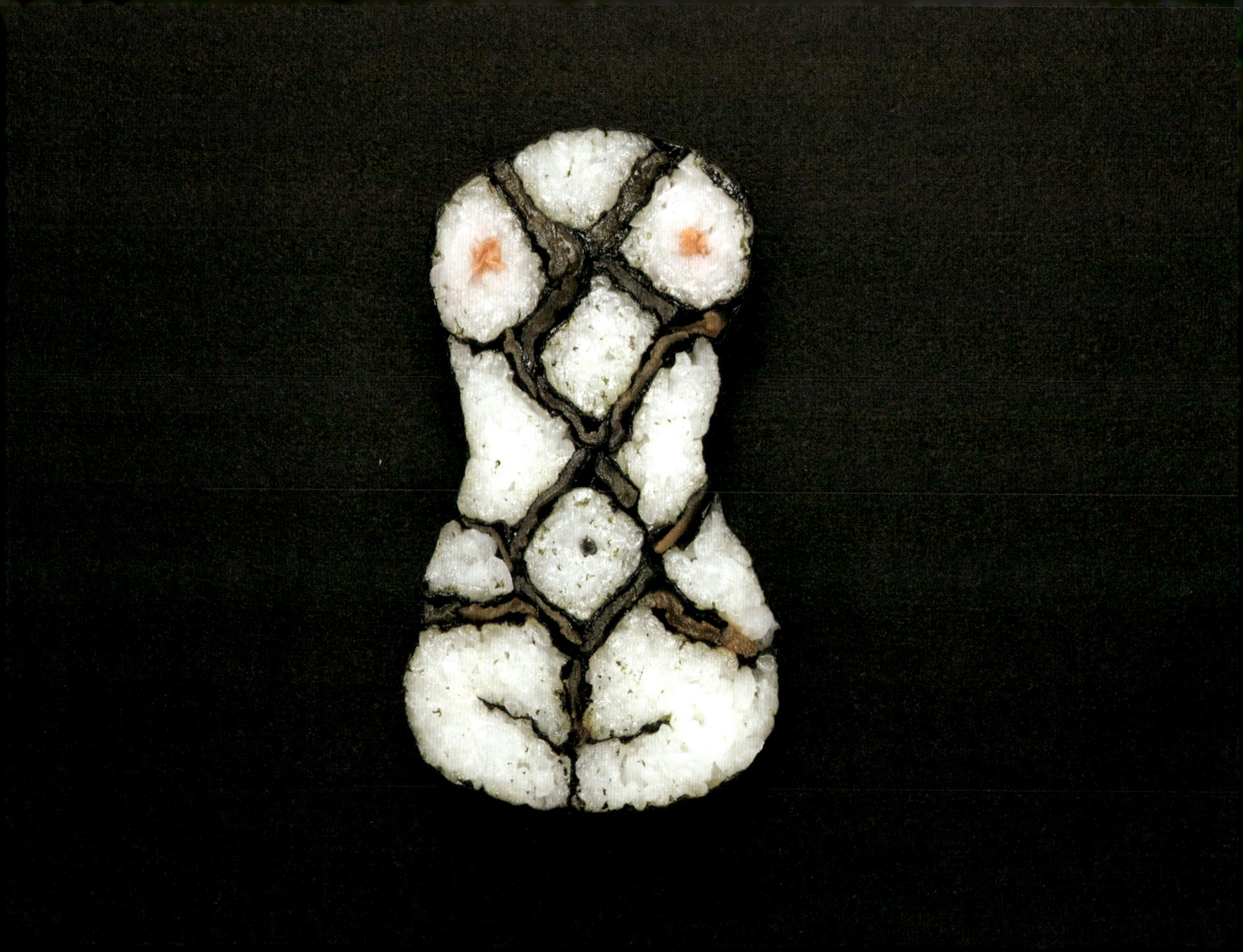

緊縛

江戸時代、囚人の拘束のために様々な縛り方が考えられた。
日本人の美麗を求める感性も加わり、
明治維新以降そこに性的興奮を覚える嗜好が公になったそうだ。
エロと美は人を魅了し続ける。

Bondage

During the Edo Period, various ways of restraining
prisoners were invented. After the Meiji Restoration,
the bondage fetishism came out of the closet with
Japanese aesthetics.

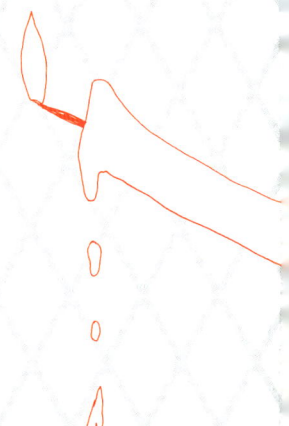

凸凹は、
「愛と平和」の象徴。

Completing each other is a symbol of peace and happiness.

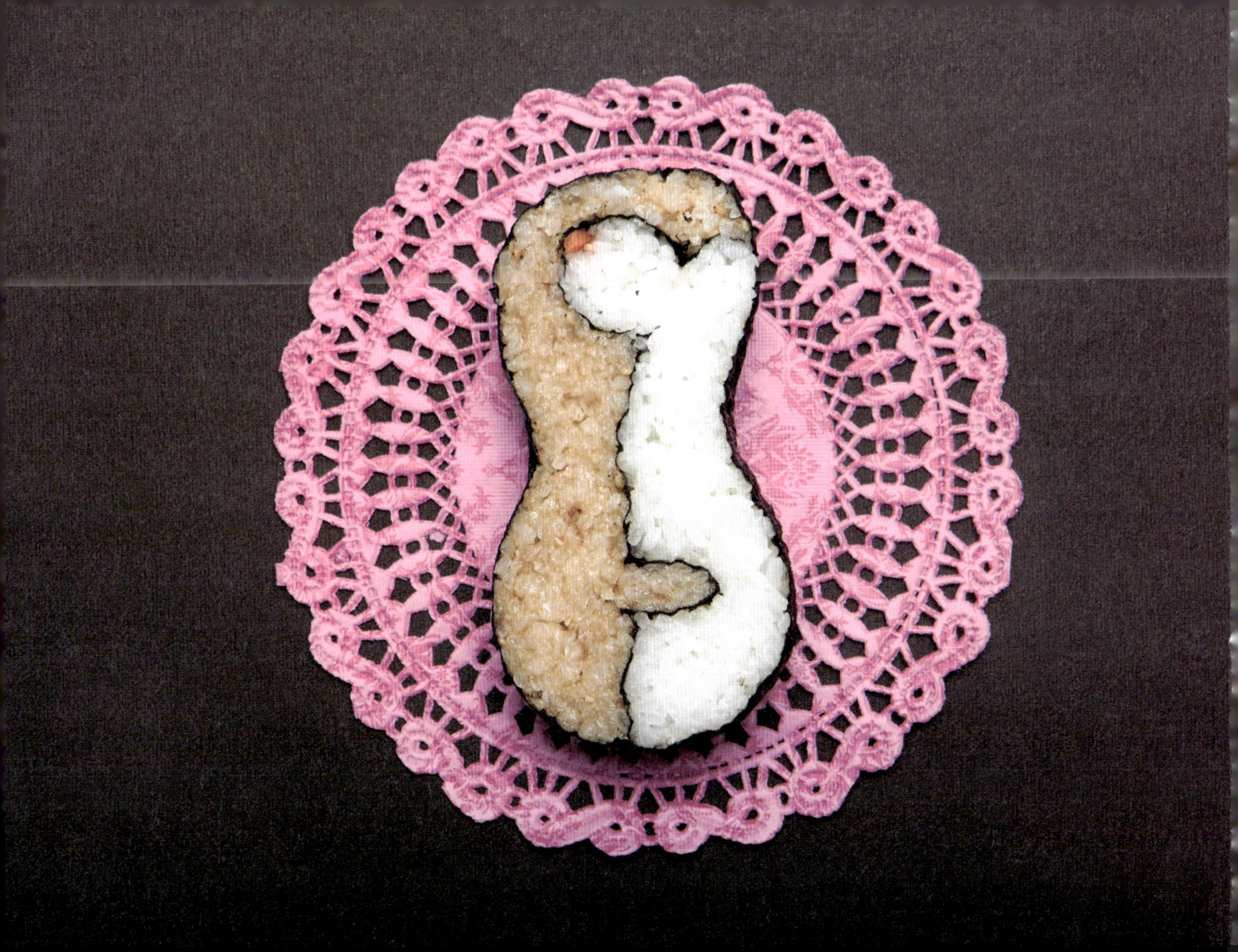

Pillow

At seventeen with Teddy

At nineteen with Kathy

Talk

At thirty with Mike

What do you suck?

あなたなら何をくわえる？

やまおり Mountain fold

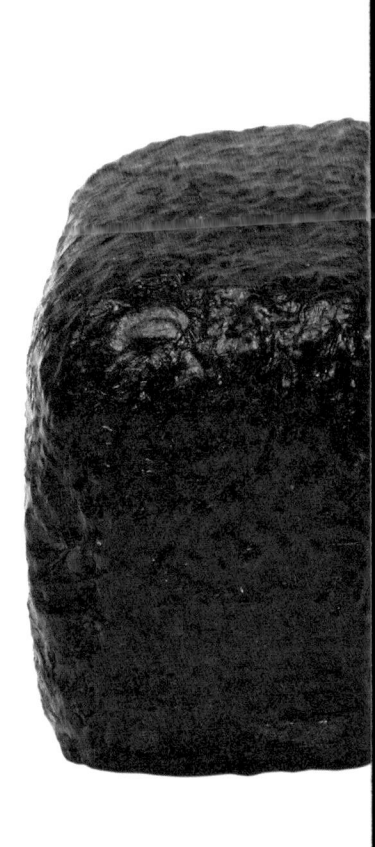

イチャイチャしているんじゃないんです。2匹は縄張り争いのため、
We are not a lovey-dovey couple. Actually,

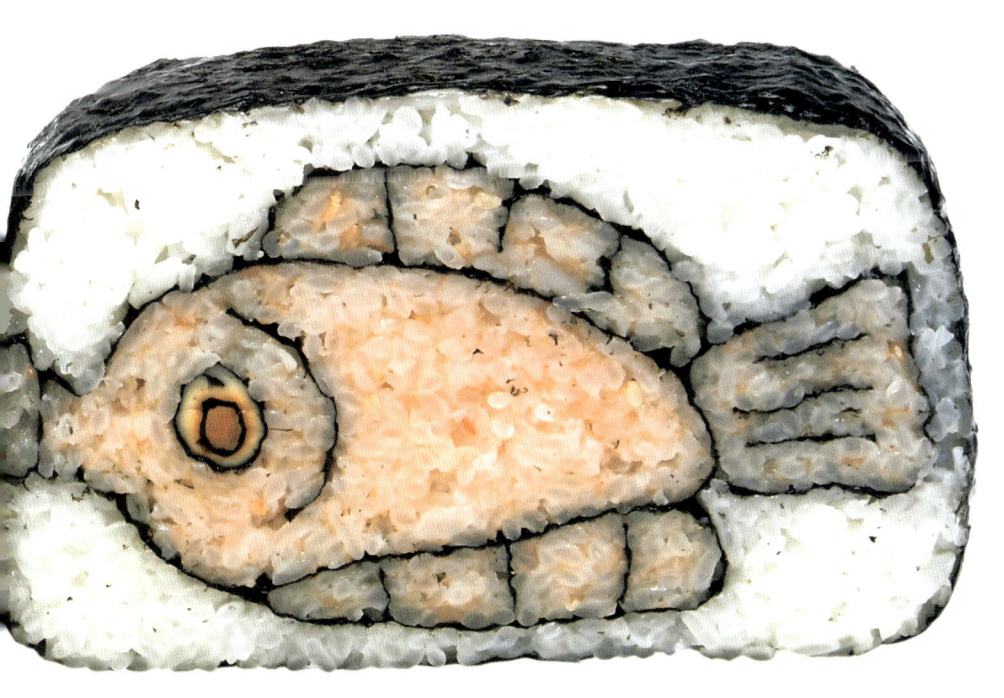

くちびるで突っつき合っているオス同士。実はイライラしてるんです。
we are both males fighting for territory. Honestly, we are frustrated.

やまおり Mountain fold

キッシンググラミー
スズキ目ヘロストマ科（ヘロストマ科唯一の現生種）
分布：インドネシア、マレー半島
全長：20cmほど

Kissing Gourami
Perciformes, Helostomatidae (The only modern specie in the Helostomatidae family)
Habitat: Indonesia, and the Malay Peninsula
Length: Approximately 20cm

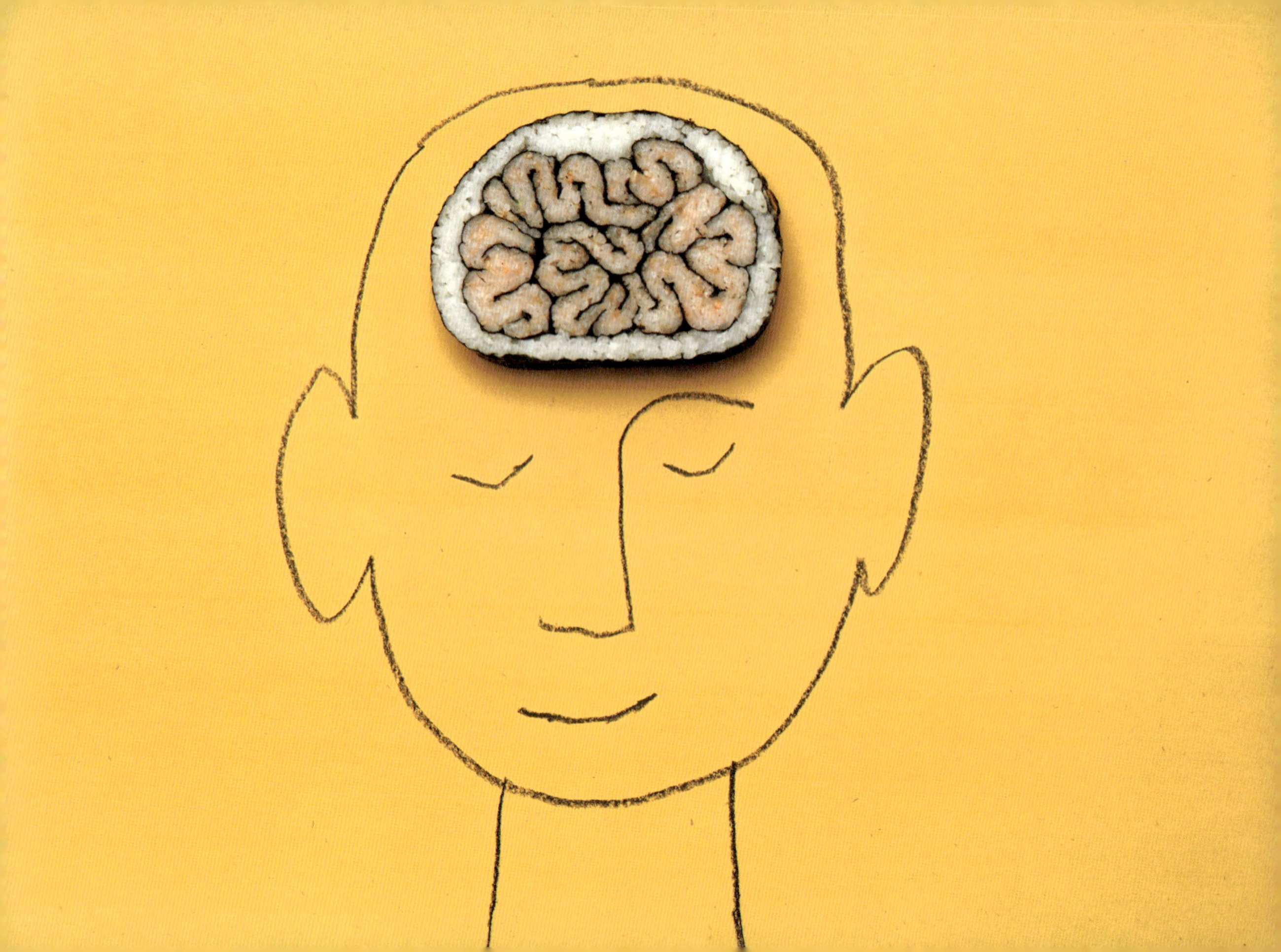

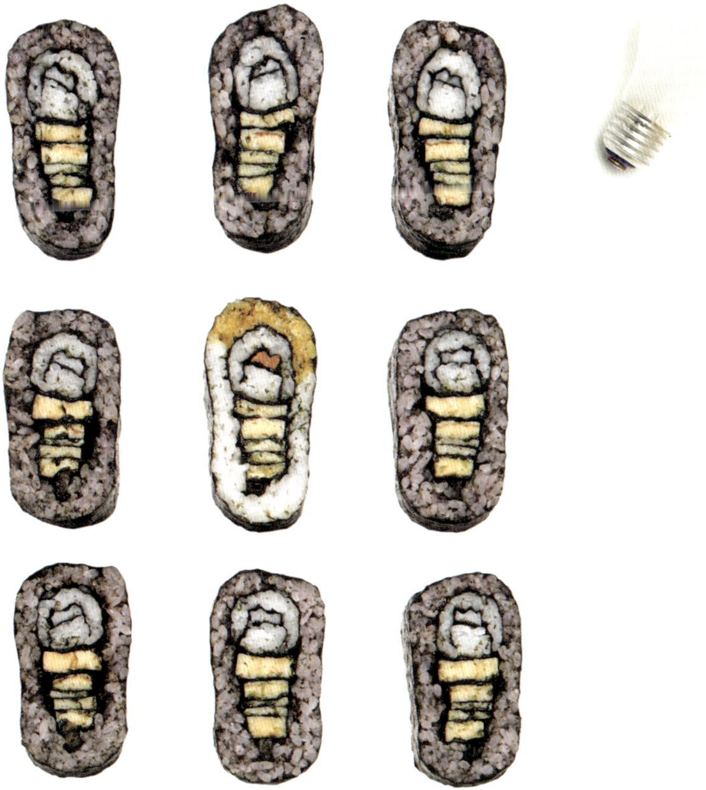

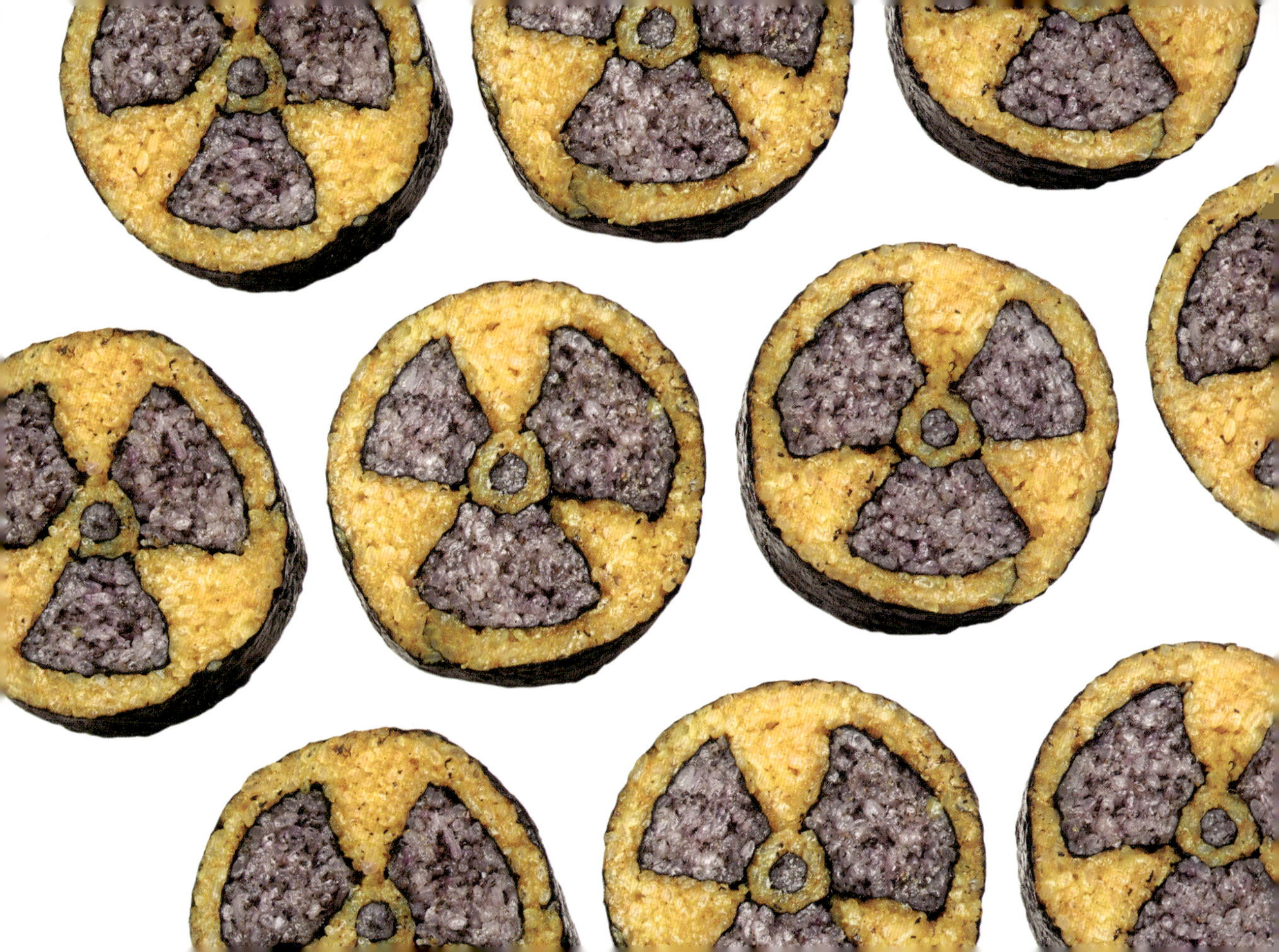

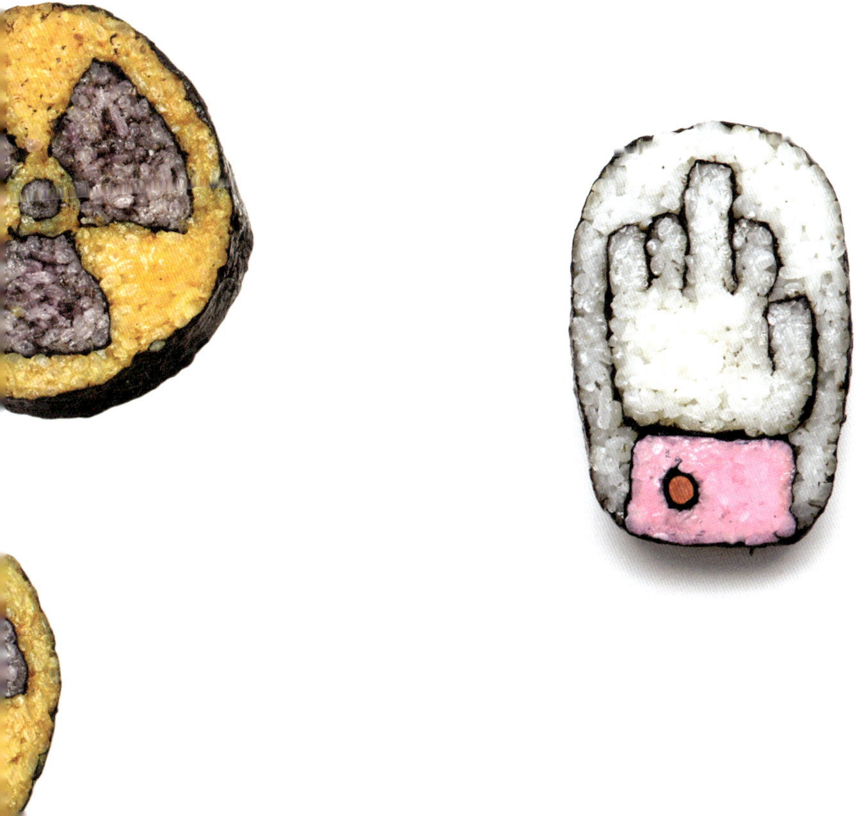

Family tree

Family tree

私の両親、両親それぞれの両親、またその両親のそれぞれの両親……
5代もさかのぼれば数えるのが大変な人数になる。
実際はその何百倍の出会いのおかげで自分の命が生まれたんだなって、
そんなことを考えながら巻くこともあるのです。

My parents, my grandparents, and then I have great grandparents…
If you go back five generations, you realize that you are connected to a great number of people.
Actually, my life was created by many more meetings. I sometimes roll sushi with such thoughts.

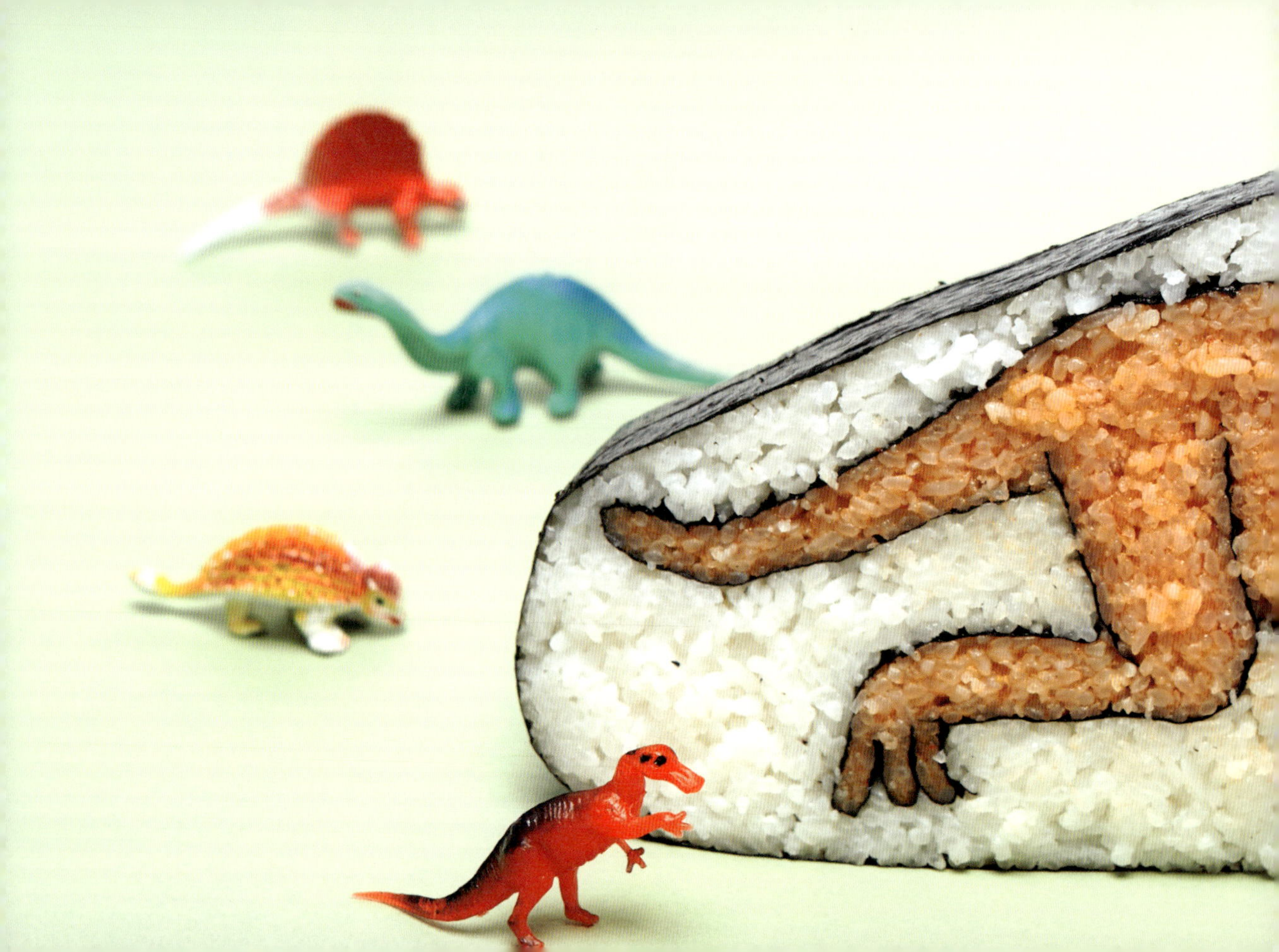

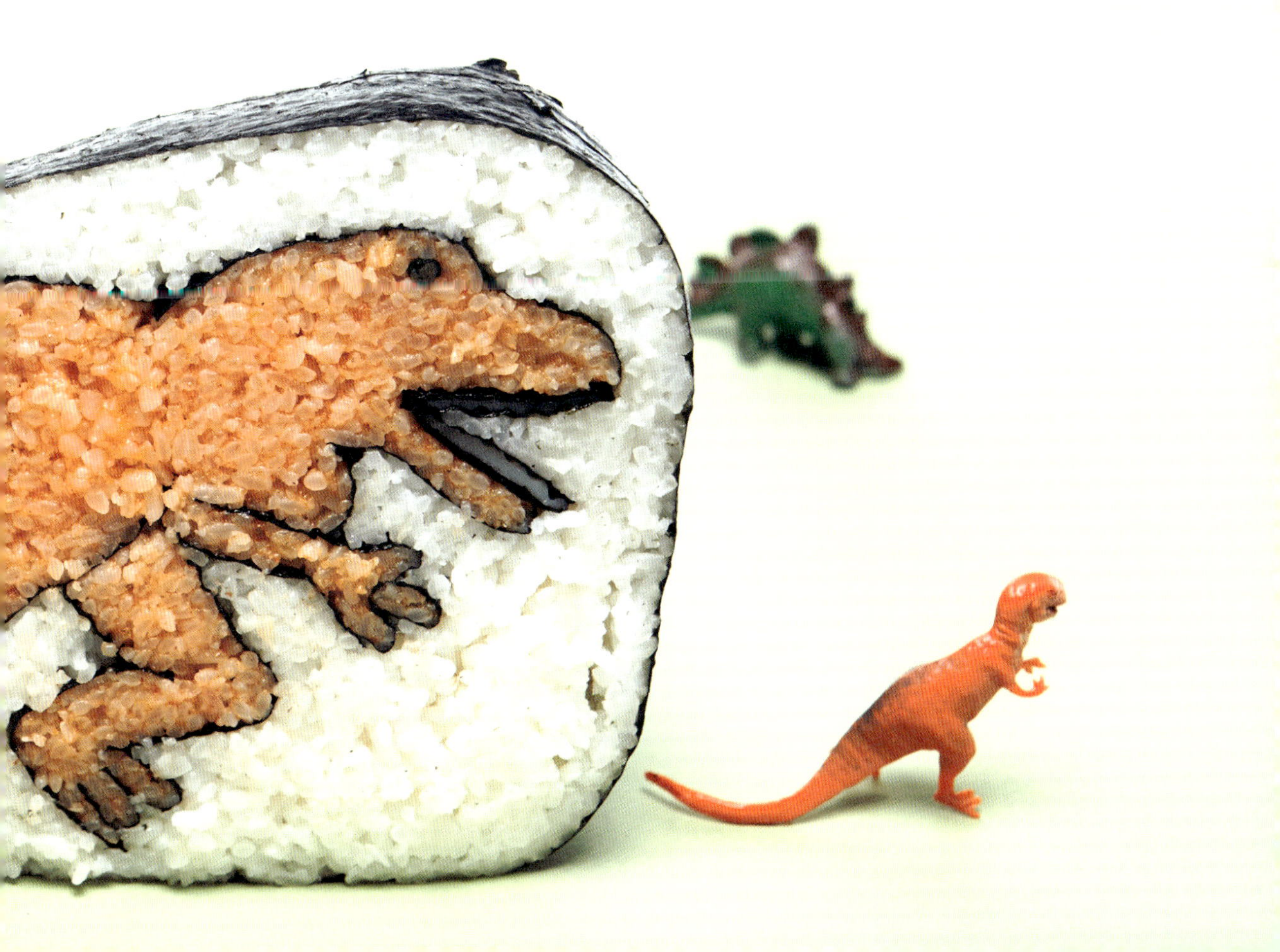

流氷の天使と悪魔

普段いい人が、たまに意地悪かったりすると「本当は性格が悪いんだ！」と思われてしまいます。
逆に、ぶっきらぼうな人が意外に親切だったりすると「本当はいい人なんだ！」と株を上げたり。
だから私は、ふだんは「いい人」と思われなくてもいいと思っています。

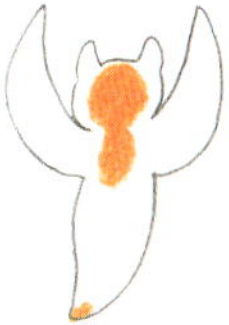

クリオネ

ハダカカメガイ科。成長すると肉食に変化する。捕食時には頭が割れ、バッカルコーンと呼ばれる触手を伸ばし、エサを抱え込むようにしてゆっくりと養分を吸収する。

Clione

In the family Clionidae. The Clione turns carnivorous as it grows. When it preys, the head splits off and a tentacle called a buccal cone appears. Then clione absorb nutrients slowly as it holds its prey.

The sea angel and devil

If a good person sometimes reacts badly, you believe "that person is actually a bad person!" On the other hand, when a blunt person becomes unexpectedly kind, you think "this person is a great person!" So, I don't usually mind even if people don't think I am a good person.

オッス！ おらマンドラゴラ！ 根っこが人間のかたちをしたなぞの植物さ。

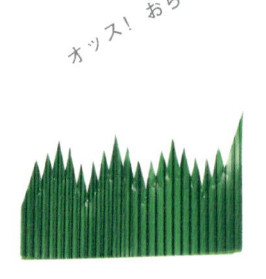

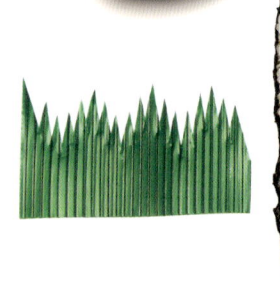

おらを引っこ抜くと、大きな声で叫ぶよ。

その声を聞いたら、みんな気が狂って死んでしまうのさ。昔から魔術なんかによく使われているんだよ。

Hey! I am Mandrake! My root looks like a human being. I'm a mysterious plant.

I'm going to scream if you pull me out.

Once you hear my scream you will go insane and die. Everybody has used me as a curse since early times.

「こころのこねこ寿司」を作ったよ
Making "My lovely kitten"

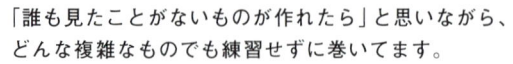

「誰も見たことがないものが作れたら」と思いながら、どんな複雑なものでも練習せずに巻いてます。

Always I make a Sushi Roll with the thought "I hope I can make a roll which no one else has ever seen." No trial has been made even when I make a complicated design.

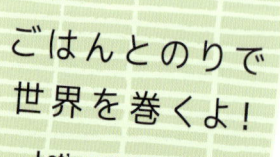

ごはんとのりで世界を巻くよ！

Let's roll the world through seaweed and rice!

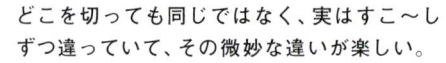

どこを切っても同じではなく、実はすこ〜しずつ違っていて、その微妙な違いが楽しい。

All sushi surfaces are slightly different. This subtle difference is enjoyable.

この本でも紹介している色や形が変化する作品は、いくつも作っているのではなく、
一本の巻き寿司の中で、具などの配置を変えているので、切るごとに違う絵が出てくるのです。
絵本のページをめくるように、次になにが出てくるか、ストーリーが生まれるようでわくわくします。

The changes of shapes and colors of the creations in this book are not from different rolls but from one complete roll. Different patterns emerge by changing the layout of the ingredients. It's exciting to see what will come out as through I am turning a page of a children's book. It is like telling a story.

Workshop

ワークショップをするといつも思うのですが、同じ時間、同じ説明を聞き、同じ材料で作っているのに、出来上がった作品(巻き寿司)は見事に人それぞれだということ。
手順は説明するけど、作業は個人の自由に任せています。
切ってみないと絵柄のバランスは誰にもわからない。
作っている本人にも。
だから、その人の無意識の感覚がハッキリ現れる。
巻き寿司から一人一人のつぶやきが聞こえてきそうじゃない？

When I hold a workshop, I always think the participants listen to the same instruction and use the same ingredients at the same time, but they all complete a Sushi Roll in their own unique way. You don't know what patterns will appear even though you roll it yourself. It expresses your unconscious feelings clearly. Can you hear the inner voice in each Sushi Roll?

「舞妓はん寿司」ワークショップ
なかにはヒゲの生えた舞妓はんを作る人も。

Participants' work at the "*Maiko* Sushi" workshop
One participant made a *Maiko* with a beard.

こころの叫び寿司を作ってみよう!!
Let's make "The Scream" Sushi!

● 準備するもの Preparation

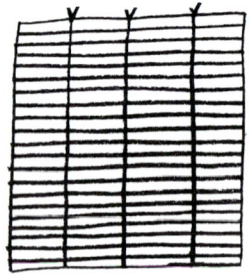

巻きす大（30×30cm）1枚
なければ普通の巻きす2枚
1 large *Makisu* (30×30cm Sushi rolling mat)
or 2 normal size *Makisu*

のり全形2枚と1/4枚
2 Seaweed sheets

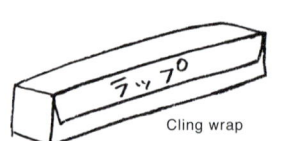

ラップ
Cling wrap

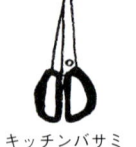

キッチンバサミ
Kitchen scissors

包丁
Chopping knife

トマトソース
Tomato sauce

イカスミパスタ
Squid ink pasta

山ごぼうの漬物
Pickled *gobo*
(burdock root pickles)

赤しそのふりかけ
Akashiso Furikake
(Red perilla powder)

黒ごま
Black sesame seeds

酢めし 470g ぐらい

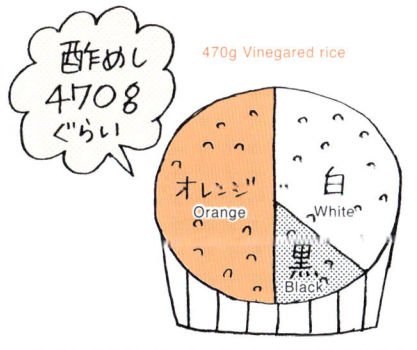

470g Vinegared rice

- オレンジ Orange
- 白 White
- 黒 Black

口 Mouth

顔 Face | 手 Hand

手 Hand
全体 Outer part
全体 Outer part

酢めしを作り、だいたい3:2:1の割合で分ける。
温かいうちに、トマトソース（オレンジ）、
赤しそのふりかけと黒ごま（黒）を混ぜる。

Make the colored vinegared rice while still warm. Mix tomato sauce to make the color orange and *Akashiso Furikake* and sesame seeds to make the color black. See above for the percentage.

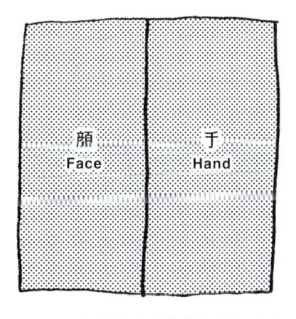

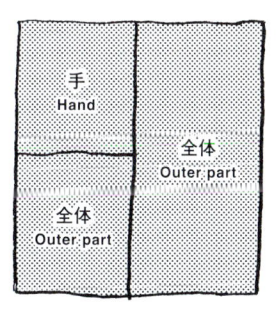

のりはタテ半分に切ったものを使う。
Cut the seaweed sheet in half lengthwise.

まな板はタテに置き、
巻きすをとじ糸が奥になるように置く。

Place the cutting board lengthways and put a rolling mat on it with the rough side up.

のりは巻きすの中央に置く。

緑の面を使う。
Green side up.

Lay a seaweed sheet on the middle of the rolling mat.

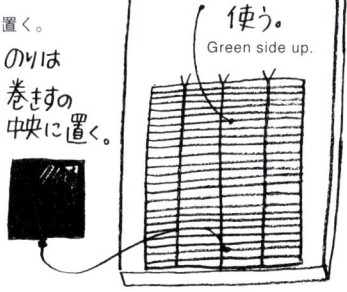

手にごはんがくっつかないように、
手酢を使う。

Wet your hands in order to handle the rice more easily.

Finger bowl

水に酢を少々入れる。
Drop a bit of vinegar into a bowl of water.

手酢

手ぬぐい Hand towel

余分な水分をぬぐうため。
Wipe excess water.

Cut!

山ごぼうは
のりの幅に合わせて切る。
Cut the pickled *gobo* the same length as the seaweed sheet.

1 口を作る Making the mouth

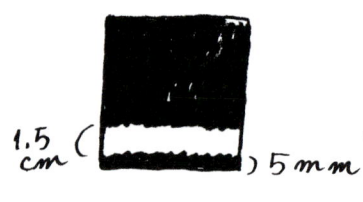

楕円になるように巻く。
Roll the seaweed sheet into an oval.

1.5cm　5mm

手前5ミリほど残し、酢めし（白）を約1.5センチ置く。
Leave a 5mm space behind and spread the rice 1.5cm wide.

2 顔を作る Making the face

指3本の先だけ使って酢めしを扱う。

Use only three fingertips when handling the rice.

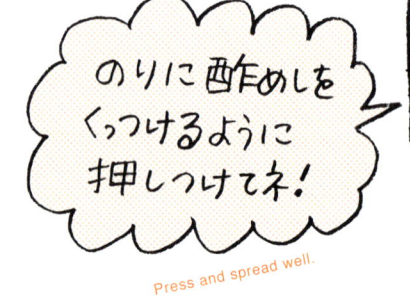

のりに酢めしをくっつけるように押しつけてネ！

Press and spread well.

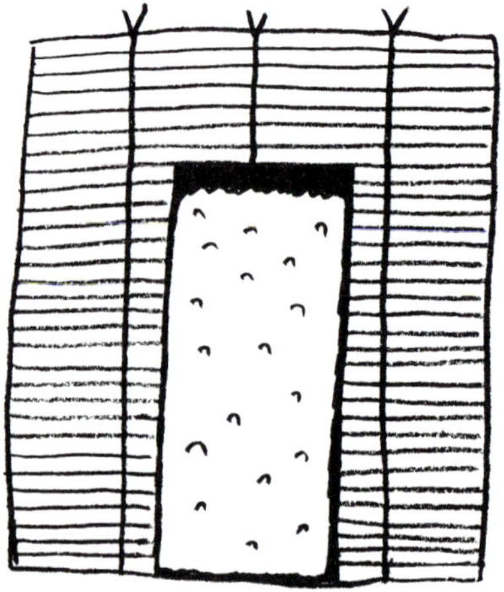

巻きすの中央にのりを置き、端を1センチほど残して、酢めし（白）をまんべんなく置く。
Put white rice in the middle of the seaweed sheet and spread, leaving 1cm of seaweed bare at the far edge.

4cmくらい

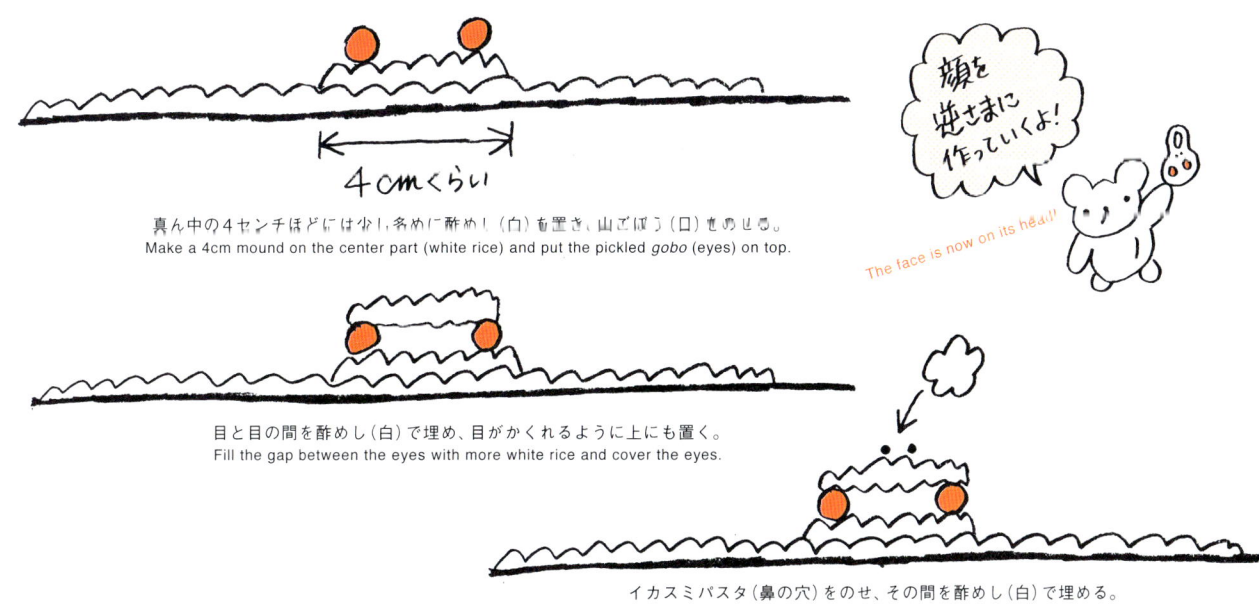

真ん中の4センチほどには少し多めに酢めし(白)を置き、山ごぼう(口)をのせる。
Make a 4cm mound on the center part (white rice) and put the pickled *gobo* (eyes) on top.

顔を逆さまに作っていくよ！

The face is now on its head!!

目と目の間を酢めし(白)で埋め、目がかくれるように上にも置く。
Fill the gap between the eyes with more white rice and cover the eyes.

イカスミパスタ(鼻の穴)をのせ、その間を酢めし(白)で埋める。
Place 2 pieces of squid ink pasta as nostrils, then fill the gap between them with white rice.

鼻の穴がかくれるように、まわりに酢めし(白)を置く。
Add more white rice to cover all nostrils.

先に作った口のパーツをタテに置き、巻きすを持ち上げ、巻き上げる。
The mouth part which has been already made will be placed on top. Carefully pick up both sides of the mat and roll it up.

Place more white rice.

酢めしを補う。

のりが足らなくなっても
切ったのりをのせればくっつくから
慌てないでね！

Important!!

There is no problem even if the seaweed sheet is too short. You can wet seaweed and seal the roll.

3 手を作る　Making the hands

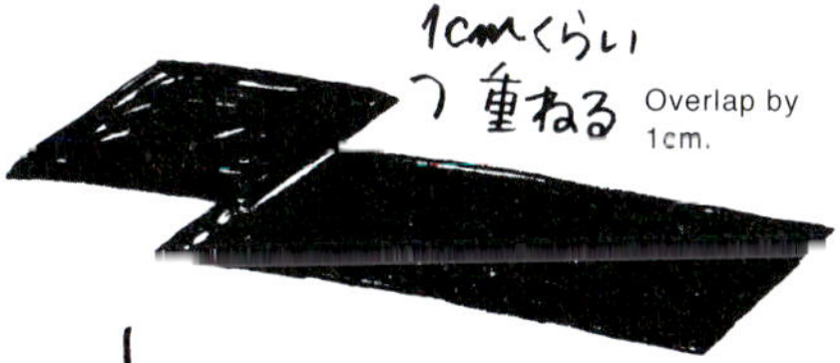

1cmくらい重ねる　Overlap by 1cm.

タテ半分ののりと1/4ののりを、ごはん粒を糊がわりにして貼り合わせる。
Apply a thin band of rice at the border and paste 1/2 and 1/4 of seaweed sheets together.

酢めし（黒）を中央に、両脇に（白）を置く。
Place black rice on the center and white rice on both sides of it.

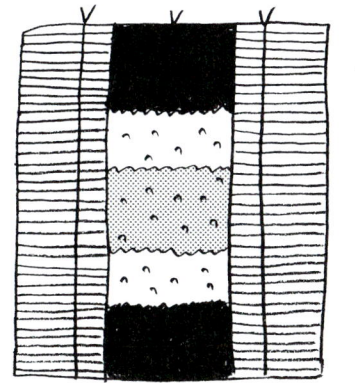

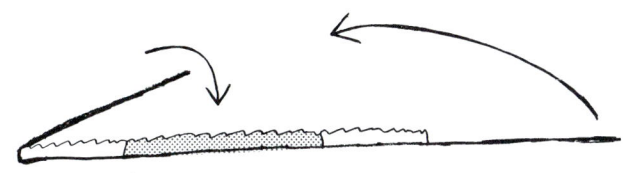

のりの両端をパタンと折りたたむように重ねる。
Fold both sides of the seaweed sheet.

半分に切る。
Cut the middle of the sheet.

（白）3.5cm（黒）6cm
White rice 3.5cm
Black rice 6cm

綴じ目を下にしてしばらく置く。
Turn the sealed side underneath, and let it sit for a while.

4 全体を巻く Roll the parts together

1cmくらい 重ねる Overlap by 1cm.

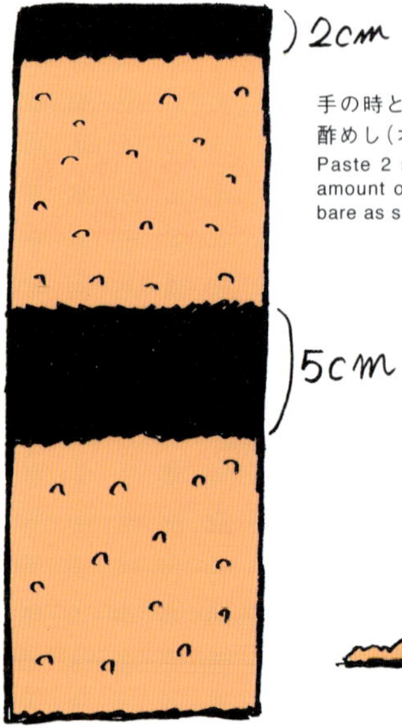

)2cm

手の時と同じように2枚ののりを貼り合わせ、
酢めし（オレンジ）を図のように端と中央を残して置く。
Paste 2 seaweed sheets on with rice. Place a generous amount of orange rice and press well. Leave the seaweed bare as shown in the picture.

)5cm

バランスをみながら、手を顔の両脇に付け、
手と手の間に酢めし（黒）を詰める。
Carefully attach the hands on both sides of the face. Fill the gap between the hands with black rice.

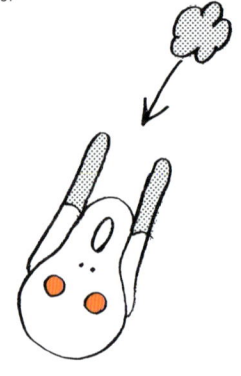

中央の空けておいたところに叫ぶ人を置き、
両側に酢めし（オレンジ）を多めに押し付け、
巻きすを持ち上げて一気に巻く。
Place the completed figure on a 5cm space on the seaweed sheet. Lift up the entire mat and bring the ends together into the center.

5 切る Cut

巻き上がったらラップで包み端を整え、しばらく置く。
包丁を水でぬらして、やさしく押し引きしながら一気に切る。
Cover in cling wrap and shape it. Let it sit for a while.
Wet the knife and cut gently with a single motion.

6 完成 Done

みんなで
こころの叫びを
楽しもう！
Let's enjoy 'The Scream'!

思い出のにっこり寿司

Smiling Sushi Roll collection from the past

Japanese food

Gunkan-maki (Warship Roll)

Mt. Fuji on New Year's Day

Swan's heart

Baby peanuts

Memory of New York

Kokeshi sisters

Madonna and Child

The Kappa, water imp and the ghost umbrella

Voice

Love me

Hello

Monk Kukai and Sankosho Buddhist object

Lover's night

"Gabrielle d'Estrées and one of her sisters"

Heart flower

"Mona Lisa"

Johann Sebastian Bach

Tutankhamun

The movie character, *Tora-san*

Evil Santa and Santa Claus

Coyote

Manga eyes

The happiness blue birds

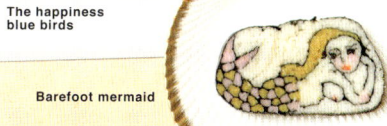

Barefoot mermaid

coen° workshop

"Girl with a Pearl Earring"

The fish and cat

Uncle Jari

Maiko

Dedicated to Steve Jobs

Cheshire Cat

Poo and flies

Heart in hand

Naked men

'The Birth of Venus'

Crane and turtle

Naked woman

'Composition' by Mondrian

Lovely seals, *Goma-chan*

Dedicated to Guy Foissy

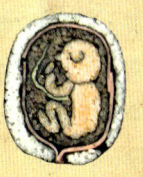

Birth

RAKKI

The *Bunraku* puppet, *Gabu*

The *Kohfukuji* temple *Asura*

Sexy legs

The *Ryoanji* temple garden

The *Tohfukuji* temple garden

Delicious!

作品タイトルとおもな材料
The titles of the creations and main ingredients.

すべての作品に酢めしとのりが使われていますので、
この2点は省いています。

ロダン「考える人」より
"The Thinker" by Rodin Auguste
かまぼこ、バジルソース、ごま、
赤しそのふりかけ、
きゅうりの漬物

クリムト「接吻」より
"The Kiss" by Gustav Klimt
かんぴょう、パプリカ、かつお節、
ごま、赤しそのふりかけ、
山ごぼうの漬物、にんじん、
かまぼこ、玉子焼き、
青じその漬物、カレー粉

ムンク「叫び」より
"The Scream" by Edvard Munch
トマトソース、青じその漬物、
山ごぼうの漬物、イカスミパスタ、
ごま、赤しそのふりかけ、食紅(青)

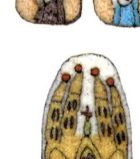

ガウディ「サグラダ・ファミリア」より
"Sagrada Família" by Antoni Gaudí
カレー粉、かんぴょう、ごま、
赤しそのふりかけ、にんじん、
山ごぼうの漬物、青じその漬物

ピサの斜塔
The Tower of Pisa
ごま、赤しそのふりかけ、
かまぼこ

アロハ！
Aloha!
パプリカ、サラミ、かんぴょう、
伊達巻き、桜でんぶ、
青じその漬物、かつお節

スパイ
The spy
ごま、赤しそのふりかけ、
かつお節、イカスミパスタ、
パプリカ、卵焼き

銃よ、さらば
A Farewell to Guns
カレー粉、かんぴょう、
かまぼこ、かつお節

唇に歌を♪(ギター)
Songs from your lips♪
桜でんぶ、食紅(赤)、
スライスチーズ、かんぴょう、
かまぼこ、赤しそのふりかけ、
ごま、サラミ、カレー粉

Happy birthday
かんぴょう、桜でんぶ、
ごま、カレー粉、サラミ、
山ごぼうの漬物

「宝誌和尚立像」より
The *Houshiwajo* standing figure
カレー粉、かんぴょう、
ごま、赤しそのふりかけ

米
Rice
鮭フレーク、かんぴょう

浮世絵美人
Ukiyoe portraying beautiful women
玉子焼き、チーズ、
赤しそのふりかけ、ごま、パプリカ、
かんぴょう、桜でんぶ、しば漬け

忍者
The *Ninja*
カレー粉、赤しそのふりかけ、
ごま、かんぴょう、
山ごぼうの漬物

葛飾北斎「神奈川沖浪裏」より
"The Great Wave off Kanagawa" by Hokusai
食紅(青)、玉子焼き、かまぼこ、
ごま、赤しそのふりかけごま

ジャパニーズ・サラリーマン
The Japanese salary man
ごま、赤しそのふりかけ、
かんぴょう、チーズ、かまぼこ、
かつお節、食紅(青)

Don't eat!!
ごま、赤しそのふりかけ、
鮭フレーク、伊達巻き、
かつお節、かまぼこ、
ベーコン、カレー粉、
食紅（青）（赤）、チーズ

緊縛
Bondage
かんぴょう、紅しょうが、
イカ墨パスタ

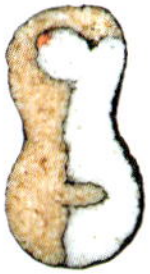

凸凹
Completing each other
紅しょうが、かつお節

ピロートーク
Pillow talk
カレー粉、サラミ、かんぴょう、
スルメ、紅しょうが、
きゅうりの古漬け、桜でんぶ、
ごま

あなたなら何をくわえる？
What do you suck?
桜でんぶ

キッシング・グラミー
Kissing Gourami
鮭フレーク、山ごぼうの漬物、
スライスチーズ

OH！脳！
Oh no! 'no' means brain in Japanese.
鮭フレーク

1％のひらめきと99％の努力
One percent inspiration and ninety-nine percent perspiration
土子焼き、かまぼこ、にんじん、
かんぴょう、ごま、
赤しそのふりかけ、カレー粉

キケンは、すぐそばに
Imminent danger
ごま、赤しそのふりかけ、
カレー粉

手は口ほどにモノを言う
Fuck you!
桜でんぶ、サラミ

Family tree
桜でんぶ、サラミ、
かまぼこ、カレー粉、ごま、
赤しそのふりかけ、
鮭フレーク

恐竜の時代
The age of the dinosaur
トマトソース、かんぴょう、
かまぼこ、ごま、
赤しそのふりかけ

流氷の天使と悪魔
The sea angel and devil
トマトソース、ごま、
赤しそのふりかけ、鮭フレーク、
かまぼこ

マンドラゴラ
Mandrake
カレー粉、かんぴょう、
ゴーヤ、サラミ

ペンを持つ手
The hand holding a pen
ごま、赤しそのふりかけ、
チーズ、カレー粉、かんぴょう、
青じその漬物、鮭フレーク、
にんじん

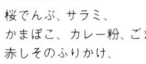

The ingredients of the Smiling Sushi Rolls are curry powder, cheese, *kamaboko* (fish paste sausage), sesame seeds, an omelette, tomato sauce, salami, along with vinegared rice and seaweed sheets.

"たまちゃん"清田貴代（きよた・たかよ）

東京都新宿生まれ。セツ・モードセミナー卒業後、フリーイラストレーターとして多くの広告、雑誌、書籍などで活躍。2005年より巻き寿司アーティスト「たまちゃん」として活動を始める。新しく楽しい巻き寿司を「にっこり寿司」と命名し作品として制作するかたわら、食文化の大切さ、モノづくりの楽しさを巻き寿司で再提案するワークショップを行っている。2013年、ノルウェー観光局主催「世界一長い『叫び』プロジェクト」第2位獲得。http://smilingsushiroll.com/

"Tama-chan (Takayo Kiyota)"

Born in Shinjuku, Tokyo. After graduating from the Setsu Mode Seminar she started to work in advertisement, magazines, and books, as a freelance illustrator. Since 2005, she has called herself the sushi roll artist "Tama-chan". Whilst creating a new and entertaining sushi roll named "Smiling Sushi", she conducts a workshop to promote the importance of food culture and enjoyment of craft through the use of the sushi roll. In 2013, she won the second prize on "The longest scream in the world" sponsored by Innovation Norway. The official website http://smilingsushiroll.com/

協力：あかね、ATSUKOSAKUYA、猪本典子、大竹伸朗、CAFÉ Vogue Ruby、京阪神エルマガジン社、白石ちえこ、関根俊哉、関 敬子、父・母・兄、都築響一、「孫の力」（木楽舎刊）、丸山 光、森本千絵、goen°、coen°の子供たち、Matt Naiman、山元とし子、横山拓也（敬称略）

Smiling Sushi Roll
たまちゃんのにっこり寿司

2014年4月14日 初版第一刷発行

著者：たまちゃん（清田貴代）

ブックデザイン：四つ葉加工

撮影：坂上俊彦（カバー、P1〜71、86〜89）

翻訳：ホール香子、ホール・トム

発行人：孫家邦

発行所：株式会社リトルモア
〒151-0051 東京都渋谷区千駄ヶ谷3-56-6
電話：03(3401)1042　ファックス：03(3401)1052
http://www.littlemore.co.jp/

印刷・製本所：シナノ印刷株式会社

本書の無断複写・複製・引用を禁じます。
Printed in Japan　©2014 Tama-chan
ISBN978-4-89815-384-0　C0070

Smiling Sushi Roll

Artist: Tama-chan

Book design: YOTSUBA kakou

Photograph: Toshihiko Sakagami

Transration: Hall Kyoko, Hall Tom

Publisher: Sun Chiapang(Little More)
First Published in December 2012 in Japan by Little More Co., Ltd.
3-56-6, Sendagaya Shibuya-ku, Tokyo 151-0051, Japan
Telephone: +81(0)3-3401-1042　Facsimile: +81(0)3-3401-1052
e-mail: info@littlemore.co.jp　URL: www.littlemore.co.jp
Printed and bound in Japan by Tosho Printing Co., Ltd.

Used by permission. All rights reserved.
No part of this book may be reproduced without written permission of publisher and the artist.

Printed in Japan
©2014 Tama-chan
ISBN978-4-89815-384-0　C0070

The end